WITHDRAWAL

XTREME RACES
IDITAROD

BY S.L. HAMILTON

Visit us at
www.abdopublishing.com

Published by ABDO Publishing Company, PO Box 398166, Minneapolis, MN 55439.
Copyright ©2013 by Abdo Consulting Group, Inc. International copyrights reserved in all
countries. No part of this book may be reproduced in any form without written permission
from the publisher. A&D Xtreme™ is a trademark and logo of ABDO Publishing Company.

Printed in the United States of America, North Mankato, Minnesota.
102012
012013

♻ PRINTED ON RECYCLED PAPER

Editor: John Hamilton
Graphic Design: Sue Hamilton
Cover Design: John Hamilton
Cover Photo: Getty Images
Interior Photos: Alaska State Library-pg 25 (inset); AlaskaStock-pgs 20-26 & 28-29;
Anchorage Museum/John Urban Collection-pgs 9 (inset) & 25 (Togo); AP-pgs 10-15,
22 (Jeff King photo only) & 27; Corbis-pgs 16-17; Getty Images-pgs 1, 4-5, 8-9, & 18-19;
Glow Images-pgs 2-3, 30-32; Iditarod Trail Committee-pg 15 (map); ThinkStock-Trophy icon;
University of Alaska Anchorage/Archives and Special Collections-pgs 6-7.

ABDO Booklinks
Web sites about Great Races are featured on our Book Links pages. These links are
routinely monitored and updated to provide the most current information available.
Web site: www.abdopublishing.com

Cataloging-in-Publication Data

Hamilton, Sue L., 1959-
Iditarod / S.L. Hamilton.
   p. cm. -- (Xtreme races)
Includes index.

   ISBN 978-1-61783-693-0
   1. Iditarod (Race)--History--Juvenile literature. 2. Iditarod (Race)--Juvenile
literature. 3. Sled dog racing--Alaska--Juvenile literature. 4. Sled dogs--Juvenile
literature. I. Title.
   798/.8--dc23

                              2012945883

TABLE OF CONTENTS

The Iditarod 4

History of the Race. 6

How to Qualify 10

The Start 12

The Trail 14

The Rules 16

Dangers 20

Famous Mushers 22

Famous Dogs 24

Iditarod Traditions 26

The Finish 28

Glossary. 30

Index 32

THE IDITAROD

The Iditarod is an annual 1,049 mile (1,688 km)
sled dog race from Anchorage to Nome, Alaska.
The route recreates the 1925 emergency sled
run that brought medicine to Nome.
The race begins the first Saturday in March
in downtown Anchorage. It is a freezing,
snow-blasting, dog-barking trek
across some of the wildest
parts of Alaska.

XTREME FACT – The Iditarod is called "The Last Great Race."

HISTORY OF THE RACE

A diphtheria outbreak took place in Nome, Alaska, in 1925. People were dying. Medicine was rushed by train from Anchorage to Nenana, Alaska. However, a blizzard prevented the train from going any farther.

XTREME QUOTE – *"What those dogs did on the run to Nome is above valuation. I claim no credit for it myself. The real heroes of that run were the dogs of the teams that did the pulling, dogs that gave their lives on an errand of mercy."*
—Wild Bill Shannon, musher, first team in the 1925 relay to Nome, Alaska

Twenty mushers and about 150 dogs relay-raced the antitoxin across 674 snow-blinding miles (1,085 km) to Nome. Five and a half days later, the medicine arrived on the dogsled of Gunnar Kaasen. The diphtheria outbreak was stopped. The heroes of that dangerous run became famous.

In 1925, Leonhard Seppala and his dog team, led by Togo, traveled 91 miles (146 km) with the diphtheria medicine, nearly twice as far as any other team.

The trail from the 1925 "Great Race of Mercy" became known as the "Iditarod Trail." Iditarod is the name of a river and town along the trail. It is a Native American word that means "distant place." As time passed, planes and snowmobiles took over transporting people and packages in Alaska. Sled dogs and mushing were nearly forgotten.

Joe Redington, Sr., competes in the 1978 Iditarod.

1978 IDITAROD
TRAIL MUSHER

JOE REDINGTON Sr.

 In 1973, Alaskans Dorothy Page and Joe Redington, Sr., coordinated the first full Iditarod Trail Sled Dog Race. Musher Dick Wilmarth won, completing the tough race in 20 days, 49 minutes. Today's Iditarod is a popular race that matches musher-and-dog teams against each other and Alaska's wilderness.

How to Qualify

To enter the Iditarod, mushers pay a $3,000 entrance fee. Previous Iditarod mushers, or "veterans," are automatically qualified. First-time Iditarod mushers, or "rookies," need to prove their abilities. Rookies must finish in the top 75 percent of the Yukon Quest International Sled Dog Race or two other races totaling at least 750 miles (1,207 km). Rookies must also show that they can handle themselves and their dogs while in the wilderness.

After winning in 2005, veteran Iditarod champion Robert Sorlie (left) smiles at his nephew, rookie Bjornar Andersen. Andersen (below with his lead dog Dixie) finished fourth in the 2005 Iditarod, becoming Rookie of the Year.

THE START

The Iditarod starts on the first Saturday in March in downtown Anchorage, Alaska. Mushers leave every two minutes. However, the first 11 miles (18 km) are just for fun. An "Idita-Rider" travels with each team in the musher's sled. This person is the high-bid winner in an auction. Their money helps bring the mushers and their dogs home at the end of the race.

The actual timed race, known as the "restart," begins the next day. Teams usually leave from Willow, Alaska. The restart location may vary, depending on trail conditions.

Four-time Iditarod winner Jeff King waves at race fans during the ceremonial start of the 2012 Iditarod Trail Sled Dog Race in Anchorage, Alaska.

Xtreme Fact - After 40 years of races, the 2008 Iditarod had the most starters, with 96 teams competing. It also had the most to finish, with 78 teams making it to Nome.

THE TRAIL

The Iditarod Trail runs from Anchorage to Nome. In even-numbered years, mushers take the "Northern Route." In odd-numbered years, mushers travel the "Southern Route." These routes vary so that small towns only have to deal with large numbers of race visitors every other year.

The Official Map of the IDITAROD

NORTHERN ROUTE (Even Years) / SOUTHERN ROUTE (Odd Years)

Racers pass through 26 checkpoints on the Northern Route and 27 checkpoints on the Southern Route. Mushers must sign in at each checkpoint, except at the re-start. The distance between checkpoints ranges from 11 miles (18 km) up to a grueling 85 miles (137 km).

Xtreme Fact - Iditarod, Alaska, is now a ghost town. It marks the halfway point on the Southern Route.

THE RULES

Iditarod racers follow the official rules outlined by the Iditarod Trail Committee. Many rules involve the dogs. Mushers must start out with at least 12 dogs, but they may have as many as 16. Dogs may not be replaced. Mushers must finish the race with at least six dogs on the towline. Mushers must have a veterinary notebook, in which each dog's condition is recorded at checkpoints.

Xtreme Quote - *"Only dogs suitable for arctic travel will be allowed to enter the race."* -Iditarod Official Rules

An Iditarod vet checks a sled dog. Each dog is identified by an implanted microchip and an I.D. tag on the dog's collar. Dogs are examined at checkpoints. Health conditions such as pulled muscles or bad feet will result in a musher "dropping" the dog at a checkpoint. The dogs are cared for until they can be returned to the owner at the end of the race.

Iditarod racers must carry certain items with them at all times. This includes food, water, and cold-weather gear for the musher and dogs. If mushers do not have the required gear at certain checkpoints, they will incur time penalties.

Tim Osmar (in blue) and Lance Mackey (in red) rest in their sleds during the 2002 Iditarod. Mushers must make one 24-hour stop during the race. They choose when to take the stop. This is to help the dogs when they need rest.

DANGERS

Iditarod racers face snowdrifts up to 20 feet (6 m) high, plus subzero temperatures and blasting winds. Sometimes the trail goes over melted snow or cracked ice. There is a risk of getting wet. This can cause hypothermia, which causes the body's temperature to drop quickly. This can kill. Mushers must carry a small stove, heating oil, and a change of clothes to rewarm themselves.

Lance Mackey scares off a moose on the trail during the 2009 Iditarod.

 Xtreme Fact - Most mushers carry some type of gun to protect themselves in case a wild animal attacks. Racers have encountered moose, wolves, bears, and even rabid foxes.

Snow blasts Iditarod musher Martin Buser and his team during the 2010 Iditarod.

FAMOUS MUSHERS

There have been a few mushers who have won the Iditarod several times. Rick Swenson has won five times in three different decades. He has also competed more than any other person, racing in 36 out of 40 Iditarods, as of 2012.

Rick Swenson won in 1977, 1979, 1981, 1982, and 1991.

Martin Buser won in 1992, 1994, 1997, & 2002.

Susan Butcher won in 1986, 1987, 1988, & 1990.

Jeff King won in 1993, 1996, 1998, & 2006.

Lance Mackey won in 2007, 2008, 2009, & 2010.

Doug Swingley won in 1995, 1999, 2000, and 2001.

Over the Iditarod's 40 years, five people have won four times: Martin Buser, Susan Butcher, Jeff King, Lance Mackey, and Doug Swingley.

Dallas Seavey was the youngest musher to win the Iditarod. He had just turned 25 when he won the race in 2012.

In 2011, John Baker had the fastest time in Iditarod history. He finished in 8 days, 18 hours, 46 minutes, and 39 seconds.

In 1985, Libby Riddles became the first woman to win the Iditarod. She won in 18 days, 20 minutes, and 17 seconds.

DeeDee Jonrowe has raced in 30 Iditarods from 1980-2012, more than any other woman. She has finished in the top 10 half the time.

FAMOUS DOGS

Iditarod dogs are trained to run long distances. Mushers consider their dogs their friends. Race dogs are usually three to six years old and weigh about 50 pounds (23 kg). They are smart and eager to run. Some dogs have become famous.

Father of the Iditarod, Joe Redington, Sr., is shown here with his favorite dog, "Feets." A memorial statue of Redington and Feets is used as part of the Iditarod trophy.

Togo (left) and Balto (right, with musher Gunnar Kaasen) were two of the famous lead dogs in the 1925 medicine run. Togo led Leonhard Seppala's team over the longest and most dangerous distance. Both dogs have statues in their honor in New York City.

Susan Butcher's lead race dogs were Granite (above) and Tolstoy. Butcher said, "They live to race. The dogs loved to take the lead and win the race."

Lance Mackey's Larry led the team in 2007 when Mackey became the first musher to win both the Yukon Quest and the Iditarod in the same year.

Dallas Seavey's lead dog Guiness won the 2012 Iditarod, and received the Golden Harness Award for the best dog in the race.

Xtreme Fact - Iditarod dogs pull about 150-200 pounds (68-91 kg) of sled and gear. They run at a pace of about 8 or 9 miles per hour (13-14 kph) and cover about 100 miles (161 km) per day.

IDITAROD TRADITIONS

In the past, drivers and dogs delivered mail and packages throughout Alaska. Teams stopped at roadhouses for the night. When people knew they were coming, they lit a widow's lamp to help teams find their way in the dark. In keeping with that tradition, the day the Iditarod begins a widow's lamp is lit in Nome, Alaska. It stays lit until all teams are off the trail.

A red lantern is given to the last team to cross the finish line in Nome, Alaska. The tradition began as a joke for last place. Today the Red Lantern Award honors a team that just won't quit.

Deborah Bicknell wins a Red Lantern Award as the last racer to complete the 2008 Iditarod.

THE FINISH

"The Last Great Race" 1049 miles ANCHORAGE TO NOME 10

IDITAROD TRAIL ALASKA

IDITAROD TRAIL RACE

ExxonMobil

GCI Alaska's Long-Distance Choice

ANCHORAGE CHRYSLER DODGE

Alaska Airlines

FINISH

MILLENNIUM HOTEL PenAir CITY OF NOME Fred Meyer NPC

iridium HORIZON LINES

END OF IDITAROD SLED DOG RACE

1049 MILES

The Burled Arch
finish line is
officially known
as the Red
"Fox" Olson
Trail Monument.

ANCHORAGE CHRYSLER DODGE
20
IDITAROD '10
MUSH WITH P.R.I.D.E.

NORTHERNOUTFITTERS

Iditarod racers
finish in Nome, Alaska.
Teams mush down
Front Street to the Burled
Arch finish line. Day and
night, fans welcome the
racers to Nome.

Xtreme Fact - More people have reached the top of Mount Everest than have completed the Iditarod.

28

The Iditarod winner receives the Joe Redington Sr. Trophy, plus more than $50,000 in prize money, and a new truck. Everyone who finishes receives at least $1,049 in prize money, $1 for every mile. All finishers also receive a belt buckle to show they completed "The Last Great Race."

Dallas Seavey stands next to his 2012 winner's trophy. The trophy is 22 inches (56 cm) tall and weighs 95 pounds (43 kg).

JOE REDINGTON SR. TROPHY

40TH ANNUAL IDITAROD TRAIL SLED DOG RACE
2012 CHAMPION
DALLAS SEAVEY
9 DAYS · 4 HOURS · 29 MINUTES · 26 SECONDS

GLOSSARY

ANTITOXIN
A medicine created to stop a specific disease-causing toxin.

BURLED ARCH
The Iditarod's wooden finish line in Nome, Alaska. The original Burled Arch was created by Red Olson. It stood from 1975-2001. After years of weathering, it was replaced with a similar Burled Arch with the words: End of the Iditarod Sled Dog Race. The Burled Arch is officially called the Red "Fox" Olson Trail Monument.

DIPHTHERIA
An easily spread disease that makes it difficult to breath or swallow. Before an antitoxin was created, diphtheria often killed people. Today, most people are immunized against it.

IDITA-RIDER
A person who bids the highest amount of money to ride along with an Iditarod team during the ceremonial start of the race in Anchorage, Alaska.

MICROCHIP

A tiny computer chip inside a glass housing that is about the size of a grain of rice. It is implanted under the skin of an animal for identification purposes. Each Iditarod dog has an I.D. microchip that vets scan to identify the dog. This number must match the I.D. tag on the dog's collar.

RED LANTERN

A red lantern hung on a train's caboose, or last car. In the Iditarod, the red lantern is given to the final musher to finish the race. It is an award for a team that won't quit.

TOWLINE

The rope that sled dogs' harnesses are attached to in order to tow the sled.

WIDOW'S LAMP

A lamp that, when lit, indicates a musher is still on the trail. It was called "widow's lamp" because if the lamp remained lit, the musher never arrived. It was assumed that the musher died on the trail, leaving a widow.

YUKON QUEST INTERNATIONAL SLED DOG RACE

A yearly 1,000 mile (1,600 km) sled dog race that takes place in February. Racers travel between Whitehorse and Fairbanks, Alaska. The Yukon Quest has been run every year since 1984. The trail follows historical gold rush and mail delivery dog sled routes.

INDEX

A

Alaska 4, 6, 8, 9, 12,
    13, 26, 27, 28
Anchorage, AK 4, 6,
    12, 13, 14
Andersen, Bjornar 11

B

Baker, John 23
Balto 25
Bicknell, Deborah 27
Burled Arch 28
Buser, Martin 21, 22
Butcher, Susan 22, 25

D

Dixie 11

F

Feets 24

G

Golden Harness Award
    25
Granite 25
Great Race of Mercy 8
Guiness 25

I

Idita-Rider 12
Iditarod (river) 8
Iditarod, AK
    (town) 8, 15
Iditarod Trail 8
Iditarod Trail
    Committee
    16

J

Joe Redington
    Sr. Trophy
    29
Jonrowe,
    DeeDee 23

K

Kaasen, Gunnar 7, 25
King, Jeff 13, 22

L

Larry 25
Last Great Race, The
    5, 29

M

Mackey, Lance 19, 21,
    22, 25
Magnuson, Bobby 8
Mount Everest 28

N

Nenana, AK 6
New York City, NY 25
Nome, AK 4, 6, 7, 13,
    14, 26, 27, 28
Northern Route 14, 15

O

Osmar, Tim 19

P

Page, Dorothy 9

R

Red "Fox" Olson
    Trail Monument
    28
Red Lantern
    Award 27

Redington, Joe Sr. 9, 24
Riddles, Libby 23
Rookie of the Year 11

S

Seavey, Dallas 23, 25,
    29
Seppala, Leonhard 7, 25
Shannon, Wild Bill 6
Sorlie, Robert 11
Southern Route 14, 15
Swenson, Rick 22
Swingley, Doug 22

T

Togo 7, 25
Tolstoy 25

W

Willow, AK 13
Wilmarth, Dick 9

Y

Yukon Quest
    International Sled
    Dog Race 10, 25